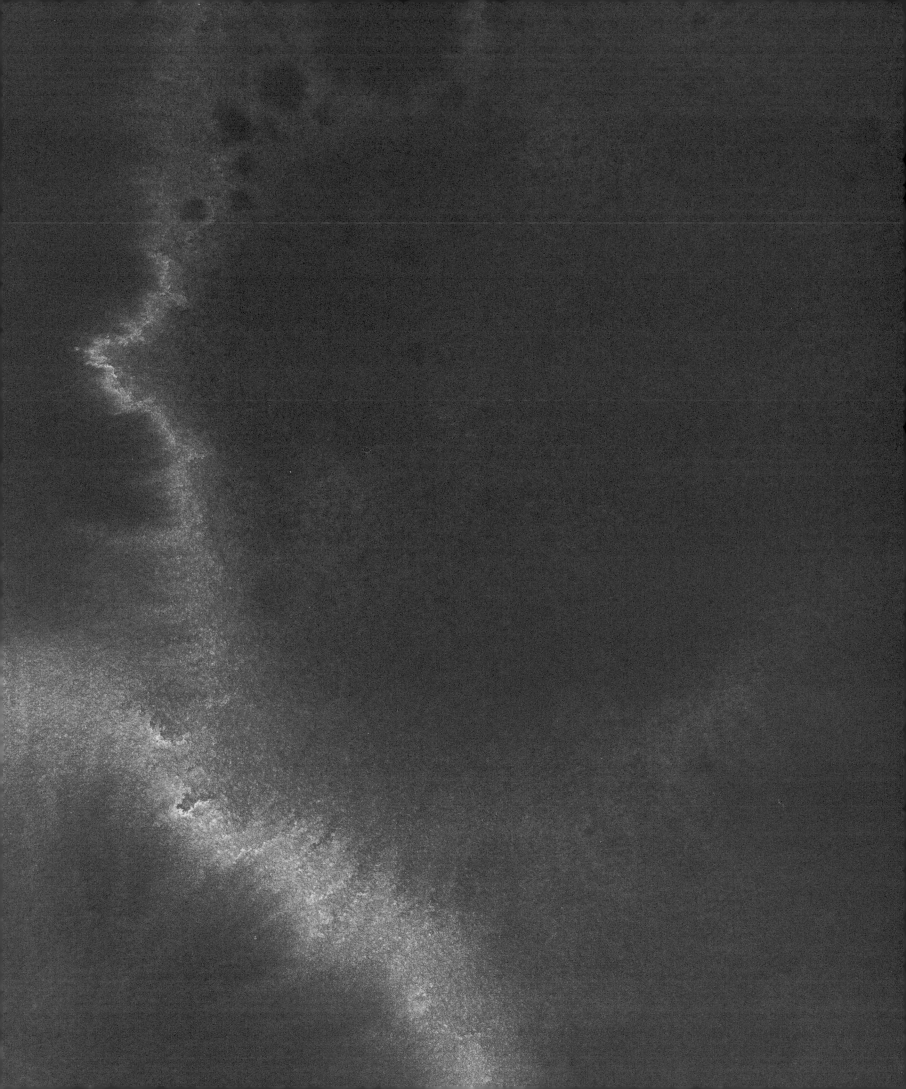

If You Take Away the Otter

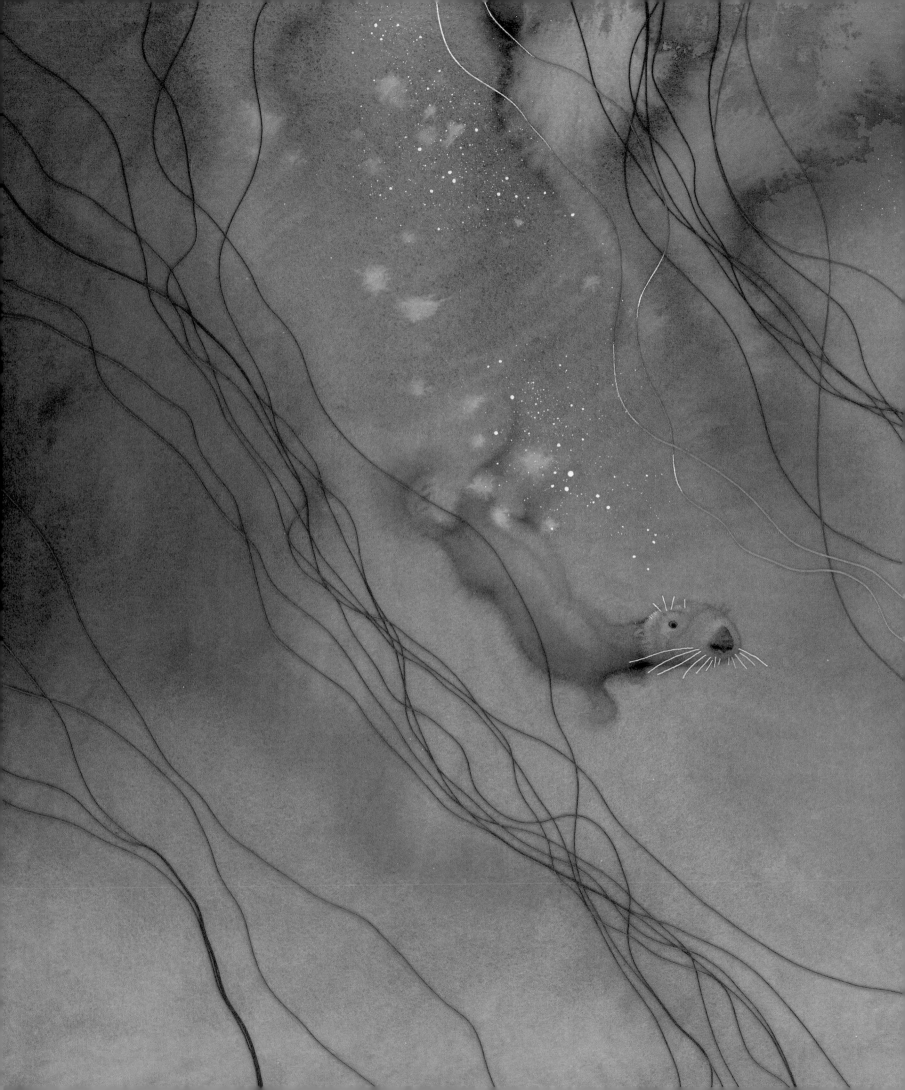

If You Take Away the Otter

Susannah Buhrman-Deever

illustrated by Matthew Trueman

CANDLEWICK PRESS

On the Pacific coast of North America, where the ocean meets the shore, there are forests that have no trees.

These forests are not on land. They are ocean forests, forests of kelp. Kelp is a large marine alga, or seaweed.

Like the plants we see on land, algae make food from sunlight. There are many different types of algae. Some are just a single cell (really tiny) and some are much larger (like kelp).

The kelp acts as the trees in these forests. It clings to the rocks at the bottom of the ocean and grows up toward the surface, sometimes reaching more than 100 feet (30 meters) tall.

Kelp grows near the shore where the water is cold and clear, and where the ocean floor is rocky. It attaches to the rocks with special parts called holdfasts, which look a bit like roots and keep the kelp from floating away in the waves.

Some types of kelp can grow a foot (30 centimeters) in a day.

In between and under the towering kelp, smaller seaweeds grow alongside many different kinds of animals. Kelp forests are full of living things.

Kelp forests help slow down strong waves, sheltering animals and protecting the shore from washing away.

Abalones and clams, sea stars and octopuses, feathery sea worms and swarms of tiny swimming shrimps live in these forests. Crabs scuttle and snails slink up and down the kelp blades. Spiny sea urchins creep about on tiny tube feet.

Different parts of the kelp house different animals. Some creatures live near the holdfasts on the ocean floor, and some live on or around the leaflike blades closer to the surface.

Thousands of tiny creatures can be found on and around a single kelp.

Kelp forests are good places for young fish to grow up. There's lots of food, and there are many places to hide from predators.

And swimming all around are fish—shy kelpfish,
big-eyed rockfish, and brightly spotted greenlings.
Schools of silver herring and striped mackerel
lay their eggs in these forests.

Sea lions and bald eagles fish these forests for their suppers.

But the king of these forests, the hungriest hunter, is the sea otter. Otters dive into the deep and fill their bellies with fish and clams, snails and crabs, abalones and octopuses, and the prickly, spiny sea urchins.

A sea otter needs to eat a lot to help it keep warm — about a quarter of its own weight each day. If you ate like an otter, you would need to eat about twenty-four hamburgers every day.

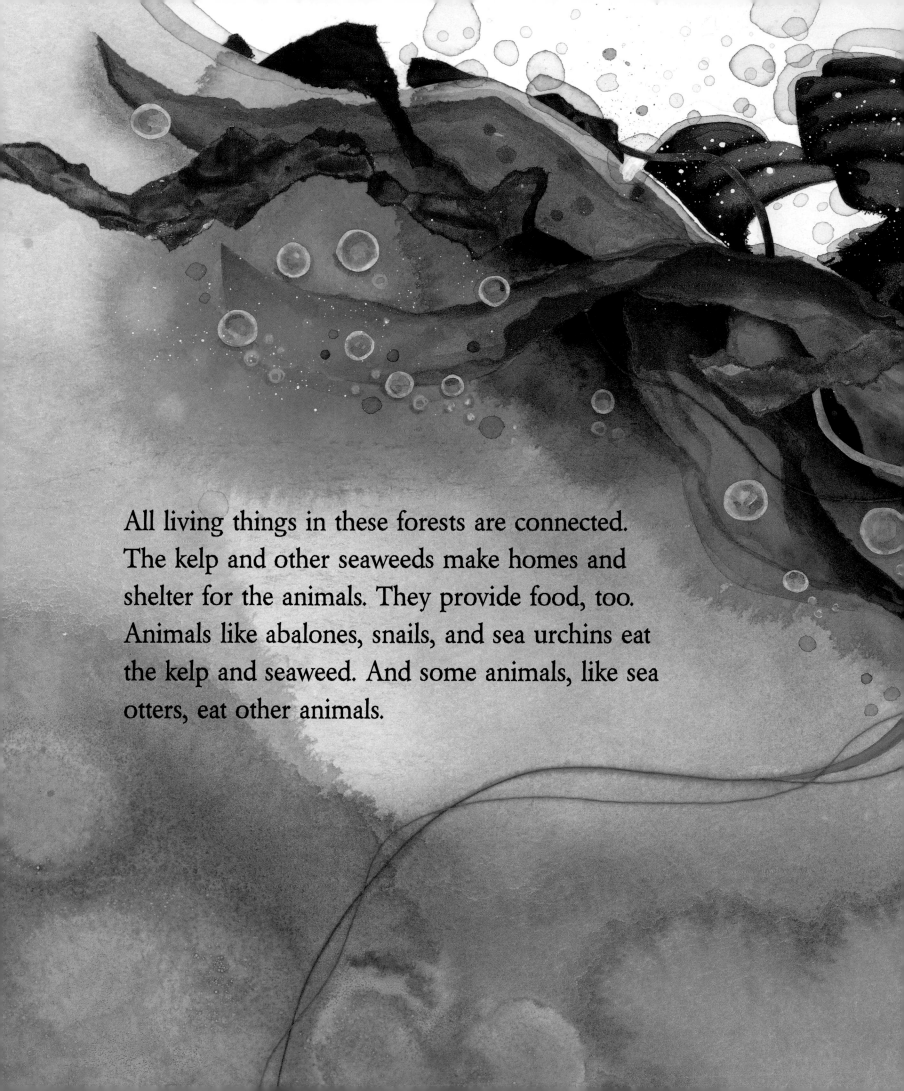

All living things in these forests are connected.
The kelp and other seaweeds make homes and
shelter for the animals. They provide food, too.
Animals like abalones, snails, and sea urchins eat
the kelp and seaweed. And some animals, like sea
otters, eat other animals.

There is just enough seaweed, enough seaweed eaters,
and enough meat eaters to help the forests thrive.

But there was a time when people took the otters away.

Indigenous Peoples had lived alongside otters for thousands and thousands of years. But then new people came to this coast. They wanted the sea otters' fur, which is thick and soft and the warmest of warms. They wanted to sell it around the world. They took more and more, hunting the otters until almost all the otters were gone.

Sea otters have the densest fur of any animal. There are around one million hairs in a space the size of a quarter.

People do not always understand at first the changes they cause when they take too much. When they took the otters away, the kelp forests began to change.

The international fur trade, which began after Russian explorers came to Alaska in 1741, changed everything. Thousands of Indigenous people died from violence and disease. Fur companies forced some Indigenous Peoples, like the Unangax̂ (Aleut), to hunt for them. More otters were killed than ever before. Where once there were 150,000 to 300,000 sea otters, by 1911, only 1,000 to 2,000 survived.

Without the otters to hunt the urchins, more urchins stayed alive each year. Those urchins made more and more urchins — more urchins than had lived in the forests before. An army of urchins. And it takes a lot of food to feed an army.

The urchin army crept along the ocean floor, looking for its seaweed food. They ate the small seaweeds. They ate the kelp where it clung to the rocky bottom.

One by one, the kelp was cut down.
Kelp by kelp, ocean forests fell.

Sea urchins usually eat drifting seaweed, but when there are a lot of urchins, they will also go after the kelp. They chew away at the holdfasts. Then the whole kelp breaks free and floats away.

Gone were the stands of towering kelp and the shelter and food they gave.

When kelp forests disappear, the numbers of kelp forest fish go down. When eagles can't find enough of those fish to eat, they hunt other birds instead.

Gone were homes for the kelp forest fish and
the safe hiding places for their babies and eggs.

When the ocean floor is covered with hungry
urchins, any new kelp that starts to grow is quickly
eaten. These places are called urchin barrens.

People do not always know at first why changes are happening beneath the waves.

But they could see that otters were becoming harder and harder to find. And that made some people worry that the otters could disappear forever. So they made new laws to protect the few otters that were left.

In 1911, the United States, Russia, Japan, and Great Britain signed the International Fur Seal Treaty, which stopped non-Indigenous sea otter hunting and selling of otter furs. People worked hard to protect the remaining otters and made sure they had safe places to live.

And slowly, slowly, the otters began to come back.

And the otters, those hungry hunters, attacked and ate the urchin armies. With fewer urchins creeping about, new kelp could once again grow tall, dancing in the waves.

Where the otters have come back, so have kelp forests.

When people protected the sea otters, they protected the forests.

Those forests are homes again for crabs and snails, sea worms and shrimps. They make safe places for the fish and their eggs. There is food for the seaweed eaters; there is food for the hunters. There is just enough of everything to help the kelp forests, and all that depend on them, thrive.

Kelp Forests, Sea Otters, and People

Kelp forests provide homes and food for an abundance of marine life. They also protect against coastal erosion and take in large amounts of carbon dioxide, which helps fight global climate change. But overgrazing by herbivores such as sea urchins can quickly destroy kelp forests. Urchin-eating predators like sea otters help protect them.

Sea otters have played an important role in the cultures of the Indigenous Peoples of the northern Pacific coast for more than 12,000 years. They used their furs in trade and other traditions (and continue to do so today). Traditional hunting could reduce sea otter numbers near human settlements, but it was the international fur trade that caused dramatic, widespread change. After Russian explorers came to Alaska in the mid-1700s, fur-trading companies began selling sea otter pelts for high prices in places like China. So many otters were killed, so quickly, that they were almost extinct by the early 1900s.

This trade was also devastating to Indigenous Peoples of the northern Pacific coast. Unangax̂ (Aleut) and Sugpiaq (Alutiiq) men were forced to hunt for the fur companies. They were sent on long trips away from home, and their families often faced starvation. Many were forced from their homes. Disease outbreaks, violence, and accidents at sea led to the deaths of thousands of people, and traditional ways of life were permanently changed.

There are around 100,000 sea otters in the wild today. In some places along the coast, people who depend on shellfish for food or income face challenges as they compete with growing numbers of hungry but protected otters.

In other places, like the Aleutian Islands, sea otter numbers have fallen again in recent years. Scientists are still trying to figure out why, but it may be because orcas (killer whales) have started hunting them there. Sea otters are also threatened by disease, pollution, and oil spills.

The northern Pacific coast is changing. People are studying how the otters' return, and the regrowth of kelp forests, will affect life along the coast for both wildlife and people. If we take care, there is hope for balance. A balance where sea otters, and the kelp forests they protect, can thrive for many years to come.

Acknowledgments

The author wishes to thank Dr. David Duggins, Dr. Anne Salomon, and Dr. Douglas Veltre for their advice and for reviewing the text for accuracy.

Selected Bibliography

Anthony, Robert G., James A. Estes, Mark A. Ricca, A. K. Miles, and Eric D. Forsman. "Bald Eagles and Sea Otters in the Aleutian Archipelago: Indirect Effects of Trophic Cascades." *Ecology* 89, no. 10 (October 2008): 2725–2735.

Duggins, David O. "Kelp Beds and Sea Otters: An Experimental Approach." *Ecology* 61, no. 3 (June 1980): 447–453.

Duggins, David O., Charles A. Simenstad, and James A. Estes. "Magnification of Secondary Production by Kelp Detritus in Coastal Marine Ecosystems." *Science* 245, no. 4914 (July 1989): 170–173.

Estes, James A. and David O. Duggins. "Sea Otters and Kelp Forests in Alaska: Generality and Variation in a Community Ecological Paradigm." *Ecological Monographs* 65, no. 1 (February 1995): 75–100.

Reisewitz, Shauna E., James A. Estes, and Charles A. Simenstad. "Indirect Food Web Interactions: Sea Otters and Kelp Forest Fishes in the Aleutian Archipelago." *Oecologia* 146, no. 4 (January 2006): 623–631.

Salomon, Anne K., Kii'iljuus B. J. Wilson, Xanius E. White, Nick Tanape Sr., and Tom M. Happynook. "First Nations Perspectives on Sea Otter Conservation in British Columbia and Alaska: Insights into Coupled Human-Ocean Systems." In *Sea Otter Conservation*, edited by Shawn E. Larson, James L. Bodkin, and Glenn R. VanBlaricom, 301–331. Elsevier, 2015.

Simenstad, Charles A., James A. Estes, and Karl W. Kenyon. "Aleuts, Sea Otters, and Alternate Stable-State Communities." *Science* 200, no. 4340 (April 1978): 403–411.

Veltre, Douglas W. "Unangax̂: Coastal People of Far Southwestern Alaska." Aleutian Pribilof Islands Association, https://www.apiai.org/departments/cultural-heritage-department/culture-history/history.

For more information about sea otters and kelp forests:

Books

León, Vicki. *A Raft of Sea Otters: The Playful Life of a Furry Survivor (Jean-Michel Cousteau Presents)*. La Canada, CA: London Town Press, 2005.

Newman, Patricia. *Sea Otter Heroes: The Predators That Saved an Ecosystem*. Minneapolis: Millbrook Press, 2017.

Rhodes, Mary Jo, and David Hall. *Life in a Kelp Forest (Undersea Encounters)*. Danbury, CT: Children's Press, 2006.

Spilsbury, Louise. *Sea Otters (Living in the Wild: Sea Mammals)*. Portsmouth, NH: Heinemann, 2013.

Wu, Norbert. *Beneath the Waves: Exploring the Hidden World of the Kelp Forest*. San Francisco: Chronicle Books, 1992.

Websites

Monterey Bay Aquarium:

Kelp Forest
www.montereybayaquarium.org/animals-and
-experiences/exhibits/kelp-forest

Southern Sea Otters
www.montereybayaquarium.org/animals-and
-experiences/exhibits/sea-otters

National Oceanic and Atmospheric Administration:

NOAA Celebrates 200 Years of Science, Service, and Stewardship: North Pacific Fur Seal Treaty of 1911
http://celebrating200years.noaa.gov/events/fursealtreaty
/welcome.html

What Lives in a Kelp Forest
https://oceanservice.noaa.gov/facts/kelplives.html

National Park Service:

Sea Otters in Glacier Bay
www.nps.gov/glba/learn/education/classrooms
/sea-otters-lesson-plans.htm

For Aaron and, as always, my boys
S. B.

For Liv and Timmo
M. T.

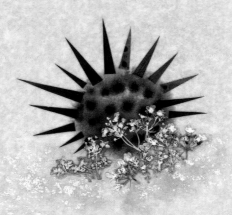

First edition 2020

Library of Congress Catalog Card Number 2020905864
ISBN 978-0-7636-8934-6

22 23 24 25 CCP 10 9 8 7 6 5 4 3

Printed in Shenzhen, Guangdong, China

This book was typeset in Berylium.
The illustrations were done in mixed media.

Candlewick Press
99 Dover Street
Somerville, Massachusetts 02144

visit us at www.candlewick.com

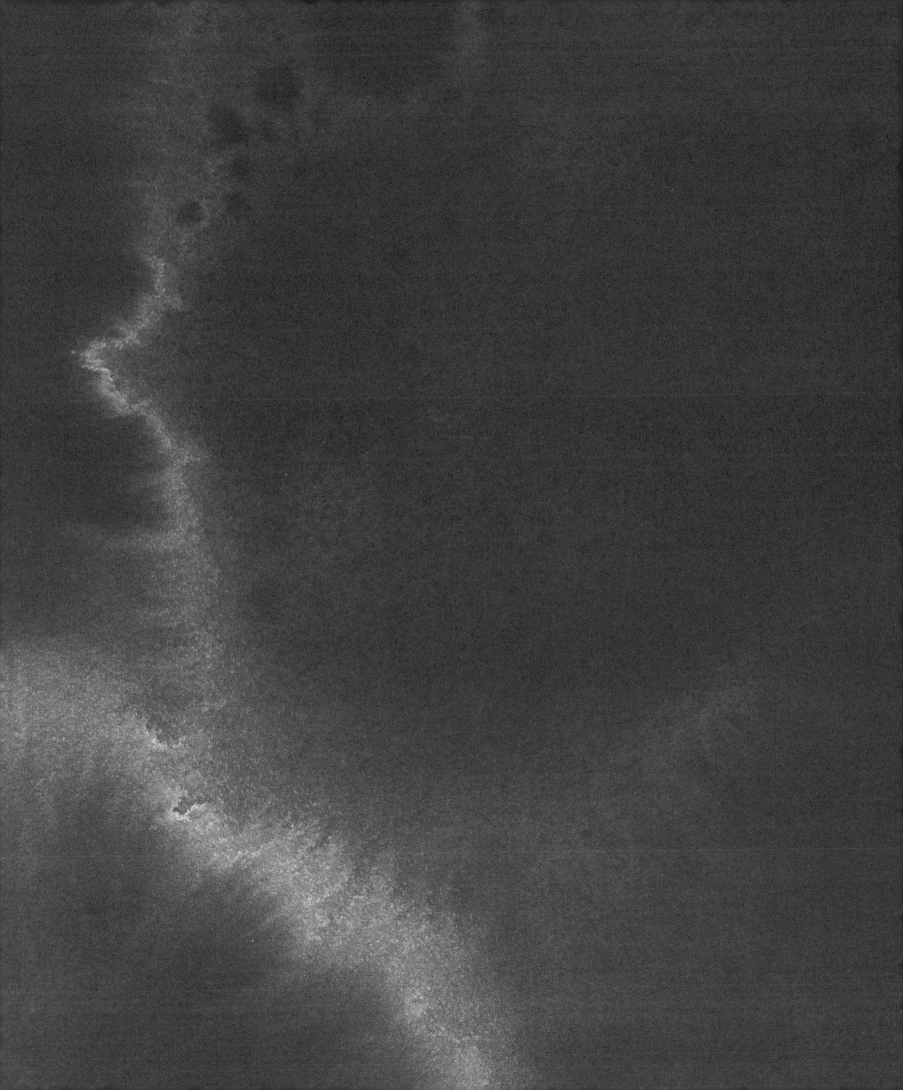